C000133147

Megan Beech has lived
years of her life.

She is also a performan
Poetry Society's SLAMb
She has performed at venues ...
Parliament, the Southbank Centre, Glastonbury Festival and
Cheltenham Literature Festival. Her debut collection *When
I Grow Up I Want to Be Mary Beard* was published in 2013,
chronicling her experience as a young feminist and the fight
for female voices to be presented in mainstream media.

She was featured in the *Guardian*'s lists of inspiring young
feminists in 2014 and must-read books of the year 2014, and
in the *Evening Standard*'s list of ten 21st-century feminist
icons. She made a film with the BBC for the iPlayer series
Women Who Spit. Her work has been featured in publications
including the *New Yorker*, *the Atlantic*, the *Guardian*,
Huffington Post, the *Evening Standard* and *Grazia* magazine.

She is currently studying for a PhD in Nineteenth-Century
Literature at the University of Cambridge.

Twitter: @MegBeechPoetry

YOU SAD FEMINIST

or

How to change the world when you can't get out of bed

Megan Beech

Burning Eye

Burning Eye Books
Never Knowingly
Mainstream

This edition published by Burning Eye Books 2017

www.burningeye.co.uk

@burningeyebooks

Burning Eye Books
15 West Hill, Portishead, BS20 6LG

ISBN 978-1-911570-10-3

YOU SAD FEMINIST

For anyone struggling to be the protagonist of their own life.

For all the girls beneath glass ceilings who refuse to stop throwing stones.

But especially for my dear friend Kyra and her oceanic optimism. Even nestled across the Atlantic, she never fails to make my life better.

CONTENTS

(BORDER)LINER NOTES 13

PREFACE 15

SECULAR HYMNAL FOR THE LONELY 18

MANIC PIXIE DREAM GIRL 19

TODAY I HAVE NOT MOVED FROM THE 20
BATHROOM FLOOR…

'DOES THIS TASTE LIKE ROHYPNOL TO YOU?' 21

THIS IS JUST TO SAY 22

SONNET FOR SELF-WORTH (SONNET 87) 23

WOMEN OF THE WORLD 24

TAMPON TAXING 25

'MORE IN COMMON' 26

THE SAME FAVOURITE MONOLOGUE 27
FROM HAMLET

DEEDS IN WORDS 28

MANNEQUINS 29

A&E 30

YOUNG AMERICAN 31

9/11/16 32

'HOW I WISH I HAD A SYLVIA PLATH'   34
KINTSUGI   36
OLD AND GROWING   38
INTERSECTIONALITY   40
RELAPSE   41
NEVERTHELESS, SHE PERSISTED.   42
BABY FACE   44
DISCLOSURE   46
DAILY MALE   47

BROADER BROADCASTING CORPORATION   48

THE WORKSHOP   51

(BORDER)LINER NOTES

or 'My Acknowledgements'

Living with a mental illness is hard. It is often exhausting. It often makes one feel hopelessly cut adrift from all others, alone in bed and alone inside your own head. Being there for someone living with a mental illness can also be very hard. In writing these acknowledgements I realise I am very fortunate to have a life (no matter how difficult) enhanced and enriched, supported and sustained by many.

Naturally, over the course of the unexpectedly long genesis of this book I have incurred a lot of personal debts. The first is to my wonderful publishers Burning Eye Books for bearing with me during a period of extended mental health difficulties and writer's and life block, and for trusting that something would come eventually.

Secondly, to my three favourite women: my formidable and brilliant mother and the restorative power of my two shining sisters. Thanks to my dad also, a top feminist ally.

I am deeply grateful to Professor Mary Beard for her friendship, humour, support and habit of always buying the wine. I also owe a great deal to another Professor Mary, who knows who she is, and whose work as my therapist has enabled me to get back into life, begin to work through the difficulties posed by my mental health and understand myself better.

Imogen and Aja, my golden-souled gals, my insides, my bosom friends – thank you for the years of friendship, support, courage and understanding.

I thank my wonderful friends Kyra and John, who have offered me so much from laughter to self-acceptance, joy to bedside care. My gratitude is bottomless.

Deborah and Humphrey, Dylan and Lizzie, my Bostonian cheerleaders, from baseball to *Hamilton* to therapy – your influences, inspirations, and kindnesses are innumerable.

I thank the female academics I have had the privilege of working with:

Ruth Abbott, for insight, thoughtfulness, and picking me up when I quite literally fall.

Jan Schramm, for patience and humour and not giving up on me.

Adelene Buckland and Clare Pettitt, for the kind of kindnesses I could never hope to repay.

Maddie Wood and Anna Snaith, for gin and tonics and conversations about Woolf.

Finally, I thank anyone who has ever seen or supported my poetry, and most of all I extend my thanks to all the mental health and medical professionals who have helped me back to health during times of crisis.

From the Lake District to King's College London, *bless* the NHS and shame on any government who seeks to privatise or dismantle its already stretched life-saving services.

PREFACE

'One goes down into the well and nothing protects one from the assault of truth. Down there I cannot write or read; I exist however.'

Virginia Woolf, diary

'I care for myself. The more solitary, the more friendless, the more unsustained I am, the more I will respect myself.'

Charlotte Brontë, *Jane Eyre*

I began writing the poems in this book in a bedroom in a flat in Stockwell, South London.

A bedroom that my crippling anxiety and depressive illness had made me terrified to leave.

A bedroom with a mouse gnawing at my skirting board and depression and suicidal thoughts gnawing at my brain. My world became shrouded in darkness, my unopened curtains, the curve of my back seemingly nailed to my mattress, the things I could reach without moving or lifting my head, the life outside I could avoid.

I lay flat on my back tracing patterns on the ceiling.

My capacity for joy and all hope felt extinguished.

Depressive illness is not sexy, it is not glamorous, or romantic, or enjoyable, but I refuse to let the stigma and shame it spreads stop me from sharing my own experience of it. This book reflects on a time where all the things I have sought to instil in the next generation of feminists I work with through my poetry – self-care, self-worth, self-love – disappeared from my own life. To be honest I'm still working on all of them.

I finished this book in a mouseless bedroom in the Lake District and later at the University of Cambridge, not without illness and struggle and doubt about the future but with a tiny seed of hope stitched into its spine. I thank the therapists (Professor Mary Target in particular) and NHS staff, the tutors and the teachers, the friends and the family members, the audiences and the readers who have helped me stay alive from then to now.

To all struggling on the same road, I walk with you, I stumble too. I wander, often aimless, but I am still trying. I haven't found the answers yet but for now I give you this; let's keep on trekking:

'You are in a dark corner of life right now, but you have a bright future ahead of you. Many of us hope you will stick around to see it.'

My therapist

'Hell isn't other people. Hell is yourself.'
Ludwig Wittgenstein

'You are oftentimes your own and only enemy.'
My therapist

SECULAR HYMNAL FOR THE LONELY

For the ones with the sadness sewn into your skins,
stuck in you, soldered into your sinews,
I sing with you.
A song spun deep in my own lungs,
weighing a ton, too long unsung, tripping on the tip of my tongue.
Burning in the bottom of my bones,
plaguing my porous, aweless, awkward soul.
This one is for those whipped, beaten down and blown
by the roughest of winds, raging storms from deep within.
Together we sing.
Clinging with conviction that we will survive and defy this sickness,
clutching the slice of the something within us that we can learn
    how to live with.
Here I stand as witness,
as you wake an aurous dawn chorus from the corners of your dark,
grow a gorgeous corpus of thoughtfulness from the fractured
    fragments of your furtive, fragile heart.
You are more than your scars.
You brave bright day, you shy skylark.
You tiny piece of miracle.
You singer in the choir invincible.
You inexplicable, formidable original.
You mercenary of miserable.
I know that it is difficult,
that the chasm feels unfathomably unbridgeable.
Through courage and strife, you can rebuild a life that is
    indescribably rich and full.
As holy as a hymnal,
heavy and hopeful hearts continue.
Refrain aflame, shake off the shame, sing out what's in you.
Heavy and hopeful hearts, I know that it is hard but
please, please
continue.

MANIC PIXIE DREAM GIRL

He doesn't know what I'm for,
When I am lying half-clothed, bashing my head against the
    bathroom wall.
All tatters and timorous tearfulness.
He doesn't know what to ask, what to say, how to grasp my sad
    somnambulant state,
my inner inertia, my depressive decay,
why my weeping weary frame hasn't slept in three days.
'Just be normal, okay?'
Too mute to explain the demeaning feeling of feeling nothing.

I cannot be his wild, wistful Woolf,
his placating, pliable Plath.
'You used to be a laugh, just stop, you're acting mad.'
I can't be cast in his play.
His manic pixie dream girl.
His wide-eyed, worthless world.
The love he loves to hate.
He shuts the door.
Leaves me lying half-clothed, cheek kissed by cold-soaked
    bathroom floor.

TODAY I HAVE NOT MOVED FROM THE BATHROOM FLOOR...

and my whole world is the bathmat,
and my whole head is numbed and sad and sunken in. Shrunken
and thin.
All sound is a din, hollow wallowing in sorrow-sodden morose
Morrissey.
Breathe in, breathe out.
The light in the bathroom goes out.
Take me out.
Take me out.
Take me out tonight.

'DOES THIS TASTE LIKE ROHYPNOL TO YOU?'

'Roses are red, violets are blue,
Does this taste like Rohypnol to you?'
That's the 'poem' they display on Valentine's Day on the official
    TV screen notice board at my halls of residence.
I complain; the student manager, female, in her thirties, says,
'It is just a joke.'
As much of a 'joke' as my peers in the common room who proclaim
'last night was a little bit rapey' or 'someone on Facebook
    just fraped me.'
Words fail me.
I want to say,
every time you use the word 'rape' it is taken out of mouths that
    are still
static, stammering self-blame.
They cannot bring themselves to even speak its name.
Skin stuck sick struck with shame.
I want to say that I always feel safe walking home at night,
that the suggestion to never wear a short dress or skirt is just
    friendly advice.
But I can't.
I can't understand how this reckless rhetoric can dance off your
    tongue
as freely as a drunk girl in a nightclub should be able to without
    fearing for her safety.
I wish someone could explain to me when it became acceptable
    to use sexual assault as a punchline.
Surely that's not fine.
And I'm not being semantically pedantic or saying that such
    phrases actively advocate these attacks.
It's just they only seem to normalise the practice.
And I'll stand back,
stop shouting this poem the day I can truly say
there is no such thing as blurred lines or victim blame,
and my society, far from quietly, states,
'Do not rape,' not 'Do not get raped'!

THIS IS JUST TO SAY

after William Carlos Williams

I have bought the tinned guava fruit I know you like.
So cold and so sweet.
Having dragged my feet to the Tesco Superstore where they
    stock them,
where we only go for a treat,
larger than any supermarket either of us had ever seen.
Thirty-minute walk door-to-door each way.
This is just to say…
I have left it wrapped in a red ribbon on the shared shelf of our
    unreliable fridge.
Because I know how hard it is for you to live
with a me who is disintegrating in real painful slow time,
who only wants to cry,
who is learning to try,
who is learning how not to want to die.
I
Am
Sorry.

SONNET FOR SELF-WORTH (SONNET 87)

Farewell! I am too dear for your possessing.
The boy who floods my head with fresh-felt fault.
Who fears I might burn bright without his blessing;
Not worth the worth you taught me to unknow.
I will not hold him who dares not hold me.
Within whose heart I am not counterpart.
Fault mine that through your eyes I see,
I, for your scorn an ever-fixed mark.
Thy self, concealed in tune I cannot hear,
I chase to wake first splendour from your soul.
'You, sweet, are nothing,' whispered in my ear,
Beneath whose weight my very core dissolves.
    You slept a king, convinced your charm could flatter,
    That I could live forgetting how to matter.

WOMEN OF THE WORLD

They keep telling her to give up, they keep telling her that it
    should be tough,
that it hurts in this world as a girl, but that isn't good enough.
Our society is stuffed with injustice that exists to restrict
    women's positions,
to limit our decisions, our ambitions and visions.
But we're tired of the derision, the division of privilege between
men and women upheld by artless, outmoded, patriarchal
    systems.
Listen:
I refuse to live in a world where millions of girls are victims of FGM,
where the FTSE 100 are invariably run by men.
So I'll say it once again:
I refuse to live in a world where there are forced child marriages,
where we endure harassers in tube carriages,
where hundreds of Nigerian schoolgirls can be kidnapped and
vanish and 500 days on, the Western media no longer bats an
    eyelid.
We cannot close our eyes to the crisis when one in four women
    suffers domestic violence in her lifetime, when that statistic
    doubles for deaf women, how can we choose to stay silent?
So, women, let's widen our horizons, voices sounding like sirens
    defying our silence, vibrantly striding unfrightened of
    violence, brightest of diamonds, fighting defiant like titans,
    together our change will be seismic.
Get behind this.
From kitchen tables to the tables of power, women of the world,
    know your power.
Claim the half of the world that is ours.
Women of the world: you are power!

TAMPON TAXING

You are bleeding us dry.
You are making a luxury out of what we use to survive,
to thrive in a society that seeks to inscribe shame and blame
    into our beautiful bodies,
that derides and reviles stains that strain from our bodies,
that tells us we cannot expect to prosper properly
if you don't proffer profits from the blood that we bleed.
Whilst you won't tax us for ostrich or crocodile meat, Jaffa
    cakes or National Lottery,
you are making a monopoly, instating a mockery of female
    bodies through punitive policy.
Honestly, it is migraine enough to menstruate, without having
    to listen to pale, stale parliamen explain why I shouldn't
    save money for the pleasure.
So tell the treasury I don't treasure the monthly inertia, the
    internal hurt, the pop a paracetamol, pretend you're fine,
    get to work...
Tell the treasury their measures put financial restrictions on
women, imprison them in vicious fictions that their natural
    bodily processes are economic impositions.
Tell the treasury to listen once more to this flow,
because you need to know that what you're doing hurts more
    than a menstrual cramp.
Your gendered austerity agenda holds women back, so cut the
    crap, cut the tax.
Through padded, savage language we see:
you cut, we bleed.

'MORE IN COMMON'

She did not know the word 'apathy',
it was not in her vocabulary.
But now she lies dead on the street in her own constituency in 2016
because bigoted people don't agree with her vision,
because bigoted people thrive on division and friction,
because hope is always violence's victim.
Two days before her death, a primary school hall sits enthralled
    and listens to a politician.
One who talks with compassion and conviction on how to be a
    good citizen,
how to engage in democracy, eliminate hypocrisy,
how to make change and enflame our brains with ambitions.
The wall emblazoned behind with
'Together We Are One'.
Impossible to comprehend the reason she is now gone.
Her spirit one that shone, her dress a bright red Labour blush,
she was stuffed with the stuff that defies giving up.
Down to her bones, sprinkled with a stardust-kissed wish for
    justice, a golden soul.
A voice that deserved to grow louder, decades left to echo.
So go, love like Jo.
Know that 'we are far more united'.
Show your kindness.
'We have far more in common with each other than
    things that divide us.'
Let her tirelessness be your reminder.
When division and fear appear, build bridges across.
Though hearts sore at this loss
with courage against all the odds,
we dust ourselves off.
We march on.
We march on for Jo Cox.

THE SAME FAVOURITE MONOLOGUE
FROM HAMLET

It was you two.
I knew
because we had the same favourite monologue from *Hamlet*.
Whilst I was caught in rut, choked by urge to self-destruct,
questioning 'what is this quintessence of dust?'
you filled that void with love.
Because we wept our way through the Plath reading,
and the Shoreditch dancefloor tasted like gin, and junipered
juvenile joy, the bass battering my bones back to happy.
Because I can actually sleep at night and prescription slips
no longer sit in my hand, no pills pillaging my head.
Instead,
I know that life is a smile worn wide beside you in a pub in South
    London
and sometimes nothing seems more vital than drunken instruction
on how to do the Kate Bush dance routine to
'Wuthering, Wuthering, Wuthering Heights'.
No longer withering, because I know
that I don't want to sit in the sick and the sting of giving in.
I just want to sing in the skin that I'm living in.
And some days I can do, and for that I thank you.
For seeing me through all the hard days,
the so dark I can't even see the top of the Shard days.
You're the kind from my mind that can't fade.
You are kin.
You are kith.
You are cigs smoked through London-bus-red lips.
And I can't sit in the sick and the sting of giving in.
So instead I am learning to sing in the skin that I'm living in.

DEEDS IN WORDS

They tell us it is history; it isn't.
That women fought for their rights and they were given.
But they have to learn to listen.
That same defiant cry, we're still singing,
with pride in resistance, voices defiantly ringing.
Because we still live imprisoned in patriarchal systems,
although we're conditioned into thinking they've simply
    stopped existing.
I still feel as indignant, as societally sickened as my sister
    suffragettes.
'The time is now' to give as good as we get,
to demand the respect we're historically bereft of,
to recover the freedoms we've lost, with courage against all the
    odds.
We can be tough, rough and stuffed with the stuff that defies
    giving up.
The only way is up, we need to sup from the cup of justice.
So to women and girls I say just this:
'The only way is forward,' you cannot keep us cornered,
though it will be dark and deep, awful and awkward, we will
    fight for our rights like we ought to.
Until we are brought to a state where equal pay means equal work.
Through our struggle, strife, tears, deeds and words,
we can make our voices heard.
Claim the half of the world we deserve.
'Ask with courage', take with pride, know your worth.
Claim the space that is yours on this earth.

MANNEQUINS

I know that sometimes you feel like a broken mannequin,
that your soul sinks in your skin, you feel limp in your limbs,
awkward and angular and that you don't fit in.
But all of us are rummaging in that same box and basement
    bargain bin.
All of us are oddities, imperfect commodities, searching for the
    parts that fit us properly.
Honestly
you and I, friend, are the same.
Framed in the same shop window,
I know the need to posture and pose, to pretend that you are okay.
To struggle to make the many parts relate in staged, feigned
    fineness.
I wish I could widen your eyes from their blindness.
Rebuild your body, until you see how it is shining.
Put a head on your shoulders that knows that it's bright and it's
    vibrant,
knows its strength and defiance.
I'd give you lips that kept smiling, a voice like a siren, a conscience
    that never kept silent.
I'd give you legs that kept striding, trying, denying your self-doubt.
A stomach hungry to flourish and a heart with the courage to pound.
I know it is hard to get out of this tableau, this still frame we're
    frozen in.
But you and I are not mannequins, we can change shape and
    recreate, re-relate to each other
Rearrange our limbs, shed our insecure anxious waxen, waning,
    wavering skins.
You and I can be models that anything is possible,
improbable though it may seem.
Together we lean,
angular and awkward at the window of the world, waiting for the
    gorgeous things to unfurl.
Stay.
Keep staring, keep caring with me, singular shining girl.

A&E

2am.
Between the man with the profusely bleeding head,
the prisoner handcuffed to an officer, who hasn't been able to
    go to the toilet for three days,
a girl named Kelly who has overdosed on a funny pink pill at a
    party whose friends keep shouting aggressively at hospital staff,
am I, alone.
Dragged from my home, in an ambulance I never called.
Uncalled for.
The paramedics scraped me out of my blanket,
    off of my bedroom floor.
Now staring blankly at the waiting room walls for the past three hours.
'Kelly, come on, stay awake, come on Kelly, maaaate.'
'Ms Beech, sorry about the wait.'
'Cameron's Britain,' I want to say.
'So what brings you here today?'
I try to explain.
I tell her
how I swallow the sertraline every day.
Have tried the CBT and the special teas my GP says help her to get
    to sleep.
Try to breathe deep when I feel the onset of anxiety.
But nothing really seems to work.
Sometimes the sadness spills out at the seams,
    sometimes tears stream.
I tell her
that, heard muffled through the kitchen wall, crying sounds like a
    cry for help.
It is, but it's also a cry for a cup of tea, and a hug, a soul with some
    snug, soft compassion in it.
Our interaction lasts about five minutes and I leave, 3am, having
    been seen to.
In a part of London I have never been to.
No Oyster, no energy, no phone. Back to the house that is not my
    home.

YOUNG AMERICAN

for Kyra

My blessed Boston girl
burning bright and buoyant halfway across the world.
Optimism oceanic, smile as wide as the Atlantic.
I send you my love in this titanic anguish.
You called and you canvassed,
you demanded a candidate who didn't leave us stranded,
who didn't hold stances which damage our advances.
Whose cantankerous rancour hasn't wrought devastation,
brandished scars across the heart of your nation.
You, my often anchor.
The warmth in the storm of my shipwreck.
My fearless, peerless friend.
My commander, demander, no bystanders, in chief
You are what America means to me.
You teacher, you speaker of truth.
Your brightness defies this divisive crisis,
you'll inspire it in the next generation.
They will see it in your depth, your respect, your determination,
your kindness, your tirelessness, your unfailing open-mindedness.
We will rise from this.
Rely on it.
In our fragile boat built from fractured hopes, souls and spirits sore,
we will demand more, of that you can be sure.
We will find our shore.
I offer you a timezone-thrown hug, untempered love,
        a transatlantic oar.

9/11/16

'I am no longer accepting the things I cannot change. I am changing the things I cannot accept...'

Angela Y Davis

Today the world has gone wrong.
Today we don't feel brave.
In this waste, in this wake, we fall awake to meet life, a nauseous,
    nervous, hurting throng.
We scrape cold and broken hallelujahs off the tips of our tongues.
Today we feel undone.
Today we strain to find the will to carry on.
Try to claim that refrain, sing that song, loud and strong:
    'We shall overcome.'
This major fall. The minor lift.
On the precipice of this aggressive,
    oppressive,
    regressive
    abyss
    this apathy we must resist.
We must decide to rise from it, to know that we can and we will.
For still we rise like Maya.
We rise with defiant flame in our fires.
We rise to new horizons.
We rise like Shelley's lions.
We rise in the face of tyranny and bigotry and violence.
Their strength is our silence.
Deny them that advantage,
carry all the courage you can manage,
bandage your broken brio, your brightest bravery until it is
    something you can brandish.
The seed of hope that we have planted
cannot vanish or fade famished from a savage lack of care.
For it is fruitful, beautiful, necessary and rare to be prepared to care.
Blare and bare your indignation.
Spare hesitation.
Be brave, stare straight in the faces of hatred, unjaded, unfazed,
    unashamed, unafraid of it and face them.
Refuse to accept the things that you cannot change in your nation.
Change the things you cannot accept,

like Angela Davis said.
Do not lose heart.
Love will be our victory march.
Love louder, fight prouder for those who will most feel these scars.
Do no harm, stand unarmed in the centre of the dark.
Light a spark from the stark and startling eye of the storm,
in this horrendous unprecedented unpresidential torrential downpour.
We shall not endure any more, or step back from forward strides,
rest quietly or stand silently while inalienable rights are sacrificed.
We wipe away our tears, reject your reckless, feckless, fettering,
    festering fear.
Frightened but fighting united in this state, this disgrace that
    we're in,
peer with peer, kin with kin, friend with friend,
    we defend.
Your mistakes, what you break
we will mend, we will mend, we will mend.
Those who love make humanity great again.

'HOW I WISH I HAD A SYLVIA PLATH'

On our third date, you ask to borrow my copy of *The Bell Jar*.
You tell me you like *her*, that writer.
You'd like *a her*
like that Ryan Adams song.
'You know the one?'
The one with the chorus where he wishes he had a Sylvia Plath,
to slip him pills, swill some gin with, and run him a bath.
Just as long as her mad matched the sheen of her shine,
as long as she didn't actually ache or contemplate a suicide.
You want one who doesn't sometimes want to die.
You want one without that brag, that gnawing nameless nag of heart
I am I am I am.
I can't I can't I can't.
You don't want my weak.
You want the one who runs riot, then 'sleeps for a week'.
Not one like me, who cannot sleep, who refuses to eat, who loses the
        power of speech,
eyes stretched open, round-the-clock Clockwork Unhinged,
        unworthy, not working.
You want one built for worshipping.
A perfect thing.
One who is not hurting, not hopeless,
one whose diagnosis you only notice when she's being impish
        and impulsive
        and manic
        and magic
        and fabulous
        and free.
You want to be swept off your feet.
You want a neat manic pixie dream.
You want a something I can't be.
You want a Plath.
A 'Mad Girl's Love Song' to which you know the words and can
        sing along.
You know that I'm half-crazy and that's why you want to be here,
until the halfness turns whole and you don't want me to be *her*.
'I am not your Sylvia Plath.'
It will take me three and a half years to tell you that fact.

Neither is she yours, your fantasy, your mad muse-like mistress.
She was a woman living with a complex and chronic mental illness
    who died in the coldest of winters,
who fought bravely and faithfully to live with her sickness.

You walk me home.
I tell you my favourite quote:
'Remember, remember, this is now, and now, and now.
Live it, feel it, cling to it.
I want to become acutely aware of all I've taken for granted.'
You are taking me for granted.
You use my hurt to your advantage.
There is nothing here romantic, you cannot undo my damage.
You cannot contain or maintain or micro-manage,
wrap up my anxious frantic emotional baggage into a neat attractive
    package,
banish or vanish my fragile, furtive heart,
erase or downplay these echoing, aching, ancient, straining scars.
We part.
You still have my copy of *The Bell Jar.*

KINTSUGI[1]

I've been knocked off the shelf for a while now,
fractured, fissured, and forgotten on the floor.
I have poured every pore of my person into being a person,
    but it is still not working.
I am still hurting, bursting, burningly broken.
I have tried to paper over the cracks in my coping,
hoping that no one will notice the damage,
the severed ceramic, the seam-split unseemly girl, fragile and frantic.
I have danced this devastation in traces and scrapes across my brain,
sometimes across arteries and veins;
I have carved my shame into my skin, turned it tracing-paper thin.
Made a battlefield of my body, waged a war I can never hope to win.
In the throes of this fitful friendly fire,
I clutch and I cling to that thing that Cohen used to sing
    about the crack in everything.
I hope that's how light and life get in.
That's how we might begin to be better, cease to be our own aching
    ailing aiding abettor.
Unclasp the pressure and rebuild, refill, rewill our worlds into being,
full of feeling beyond measure.
When your storm feels too hard, too harsh to weather,
    remember: *kintsugi*.
The art of building beauty from that which has been broken,
repairing the ruptures until at last they gleam golden.
Where mirth and dirge converge
the worst, the hurtling verge, the hurts are interwoven.
Not hidden, left showing, exposing the past of the pottery,
the cracks in the crockery,
the flawed and the tortured, the confident and cautious, the gaps
    and the gapes,
the tragic mistakes that we fit back into place, reshape, glue into
    gorgeous.
So forfeit the thought of being flawless, find the sacred in your scars,
don't be marred by the marks or the masks you have hidden behind.

---

1   Kintsugi (noun): The art of repairing pottery with gold or silver
lacquer and understanding that the piece is more beautiful for having
been broken.

Stand adoring at the altar of being alive,
of keeping the courage to sustain yourself and survive.
Strengthen your not-your-fault lines until your majesty shines.
Your vicious incisions in your soft-skinned arms, your beating heart,
    your precious, restless mind.
Give them time.
Restitch the seams, extend and expend your care to every piece of
    your being.
Stay seeking the season of your soul,
stay believing in your bones.
Embrace this holy unfolding, find comfort consoling in knowing you
    are wholly wholeheartedly whole.
For everything grows.
Nothing is forever inevitably sterile and stagnant.
Life can be built out of dazzling filigreed fragments.

OLD AND GROWING

On the day that you plucked the first whispering white hair from
    your head,
you said,
'I am scared of growing older and greying, ungracefully, shamefully
    decaying.'
I replied that I am not scared of growing old.
I am scared of not growing old, of choosing to leave my story untold.
I want to be old and growing.
I want to be more open, more self-owning,
less prone to demoting, disavowing, disowning the worth that I have
    in this world.
I want to know myself, show myself that I matter,
be enwrapped and enraptured in self-knowledge, curled up in my
    courage.
I want to ferment and to mend and to thoroughly flourish.
I want to extol the virtue of age,
the wisdom gained, the mistakes borne with grace.
I want to get to a place
where I can shake off the shadows and the shame from my soul,
feel at home inside my own skin.
I want to celebrate its stretch marks and stress lines and the signs of
    the things that this body has been.
Its restless renewals, its ability to re-begin.
I want to applaud its resilience,
bask in this bodily brilliance.
I want to trace its changes, praise its lack of stasis, track and chart its
    phases, see its stages, sing this self I've self-curated,
see the quelling of its storm,
see it reborn to self-worth from long-borne,
long drawn   out,
well-worn,
well worn out self-hatred.
I want to feel shameless in the process of aging.
I want to rage, rage, rage against the dyeing of my hair,
I want to go ungentle, inconstant, temperamental into
a more mature, enormous, dawnless, gorgeous night.
I want a brighter life,
a more assured, a more fully formed, informed, less forlorn
    and torn mind.
I want (and want for) time.

I want time to just settle, to rip apart and reassemble,
to refuse and refute this cultish, chronic obsession with youth.
I want the small setbacks to not rip me asunder.
I want to be stronger.
I want to unwaveringly wander and wonder in my confidence,
I want looking younger than you actually are to not be compliment.
I want to be treated the same as the men,
I want to, like them, have my age and the way I look signal authority,
a kind of profundity,
not a cultural redundancy, reserved for women beyond
        the point of fecundity.
I want to see older women represented,
commended for their histories, their tiny and towering victories,
        their defining defeats, their rising feats, the things they've
        achieved, their courage, their candour,
the hammers they've hurled at glass ceilings, the stories that
        sing in their beings.
I want to be set alight, inspired to fight by their might and their
        meaning.
I want to breathe in, believe in defiant, defining, not declining years,
golden and gorgeous and glowing.
I hope to cope, to keep myself going, to be old and greying
        and growing.

INTERSECTIONALITY

'When we don't pay attention to the margins, when we don't acknowledge the intersection, where the places of power overlap, we not only fail to see the women who fall between our movements, sometimes we pit our movements against each other.'

Kimberlé Crenshaw

I think it's unacceptable to not be intersectional.
To not think how things oppress us all in different ways.
How not all of us face a struggle for our religion or race,
for our gender identity, mental health history,
for the people we love or the things that we say.
Where our paths cross, let that be our way.
Know how much space you take up.
Open your mind and wake up to the worlds worn by other women.
Don't speak over, listen.
Fight bright, defiant for those who are most a vicious society's victim.
Remain indignant, not indifferent, stand with them, bear witness.
Look after every kind,
every fellow mind,
every one of your sisters.

RELAPSE

It happens out of nowhere.
In the kind of situation that isn't actually ironic,
but the kind of situation Alanis Morissette would profess was ironic.
A misstep, a mishap, a mistake, a minute.
In the instant, in the innocuous, you feel once again the chronic,
the toxic full-thick fog of it,
the nauseous, noxious nothingness.
You do not know how it happens, to be honest,
but you are locked in the toilet cubicle weeping.
You are weeping because the sadness has seeped in again.
You are weeping in the middle of a meeting.
You are weeping your way along the Strand.
You are weeping so hard you're barely breathing.
You are weeping at a party, to your partner.
You are weeping and walking through the darkness.
You are weeping in a bar sat alone surrounded by people.
You are weeping in the waiting room.
You are weeping for weeks on end to your therapist.
You are weeping for the endlessness of it.
You are weeping for six days, buried under a duvet,
unable to open your curtains.
You are weeping at work.
You are weeping because you are not working.
You are weeping because you are worthless.
You are weeping because you feel that all you are is a burden.
You are weeping without purpose.
You are not weeping on purpose.
You are weeping without a reason you can divine.
You are weeping because you do not want to die.
You are weeping without knowing why you need to cry.
You are weeping until it's keeping you from sleeping.
You are repeating and repeating and repeating.
You are weeping for the courage to try, defy and counteract
the taxing attack,
the crippling setback,
    the
    crush
    of
    collapse.
You are weeping because once again you have relapsed.

NEVERTHELESS, SHE PERSISTED.

'She was warned. She was given an explanation.
Nevertheless, she persisted.'

Senator Mitch McConnell, of Senator Elizabeth Warren

I am good at shutting up, buttoning up, not butting in, not speaking.
Feeling furtive and flawed, concealing, deleting my thoughts,
not championing my cause in meetings, sitting decidedly mute.
Letting my inner patriarch rule,
constricting and cruel:
'You stupid fool, full of useless, fruitless thoughts,'
the tireless taunt beneath my skin, that teaches me to keep my
    innards in.
I have mastered learning to shrink,
learning to think that speech is the business of men.
I surrender to the endless, distended, discouraging sentences that
    sentence my self to silence, to my inner self-violence.
Yet I long to rise riotous with righteousness, defy my quietness.
For the sound of silencing is already there
in our heads.
Already practised by men
in the house, in the senate, in the seminar,
in the cells, in the cities, in the streets, in the President's tweets,
the festering fear of letting women speak.
So let our symphony sing free and let them hear our demands.
For I stand with my per*sisters*, my an*sisters*, re*sisters*,
the glass ceiling chisellers, the outspoken ministers, the victors
    invictus.
I stand with the petitioners, the political prisoners visioning new
    vistas into existence.
I stand with those who have risen, with the valiant un-victimed,
with the restless and resilient, censured and censored civilians.
I stand with women in their millions whose lives we rewrite or deny
    or let live unlistened.
I stand in resistance with every race and religion,
against every face erased, each countless omission, each figure left
    hidden, each edition, each missive missile missing from the
    archives of our history.
I stand persistent, sisterly, insistently.

Like Warren warned in the Senate, I stand relentless, not
    defenceless, with every distant an*sister* so garrulous and gifted,
every ban they have lifted,
every sentence they have finished, defiant and distinguished,
    undiminished.
For though they sought to oppress:
nevertheless, she persisted.

E

ıld.

ay TV.

...ash Hits, 'Hit Me Baby One More Time'.

Britney!

The one, the blonde, I'd like to be.

I try to morph her into me.

Pretend my three-foot-four and two left feet can bounce and bend
     as good as she.

I try to do *that* slick high kick at the end of the vid that Brit just did.

But I've been tricked.

I miss.

I hit my baby face one more time and now I am bleeding.

Really, really bleeding.

Weeping, head back, troubled bridge held over kitchen sink water.

And I ought to have known that these gender roles we're shown
     mean that we can never win.

They are sewn into our skin from the day that we begin like name
     tags in school uniform,

whilst sixteen-year-old Brit wearing hers must perform

the short-skirt sexy schoolgirl routine, surrounded by full-clothed
     men who have long left their teens.

I continue to bleed.

Yet still my eyes rest, glued to the screen.

Because it is 1998 and I am five and yet to discover that sexism exists,

and I just want to be Brit, to not have to sit inside the skin of a body

which already offers me shame that pervades every sinew,

clothes that I do not fit into,

a lack of confidence and courage to continue in a world in which I
     already know

it proves fruitful to be elastically, ecstatically, fantastically, fanatically
     beautiful.

I am the dutiful receiver of this image of women, young girls high
     kicking

that I will never be able to copy, and I shouldn't let that stop me

from feeling self-worth.

I want to learn to be a girl and not yet a woman in a world where we
     constantly count calories, shove spears in our sanities until we
     look like the Britney that all of us can't be.

For, beautiful and brilliant as she may be, she is she and me is me.
That was the day I began to see that sexism tastes like swallowing
Coco Pops, unrealistic beauty standards and buckets full of
blood on a Saturday morning in 1998.
I try to sing a different song,
for bleeding gives me a sign, not to hit my baby face one more time.

DISCLOSURE

I have a mental illness.
I bear it, bare it, wear it not as a badge of honour
but as a badge of honest.
A shameless sonnet, an unconquered kingdom,
the gin, the sting (ma)lingering beneath the skin without a tonic.
I will not keep it in a closet.
I promise to be a persister,
escaping your stigma, reclaiming proclaiming my sickness,
repainting the picture, landscaping, reshaping my vistas.
This is something I will live through and live with.
Not without medical assistance, not without pain and shame and
        indifference,
not without therapy, not without an internal enemy,
but I intend to be
restlessly, relentlessly, immensely, tremendously and splendidly
unpretending.
Free, for every possible precious minute.
I have more, I am more than my mental illness.

DAILY MALE

He tells me,
'When you are older, you won't think like that!
Your head will not be full of socialist crap, you'll eschew the ideals
    of your youth, you too will want your own country back.
You'll respect Mrs Thatcher.
You will attack pacifistic action; you will be a dedicated swallower
    of fascism.
You will not care about what's actually happening.
You will seek your "facts" from factions.
You will not hold your government accountable for their actions.
You won't care which companies pay their taxes, in practice it
    doesn't matter.
You'll have selective compassion during human disasters.
You'll want "scroungers" and "immigrants" deported faster.
You'll be able to "banter" with conviction.
You too will taunt women,
especially the ones who are given to "flaunting" their flesh in public
    settings.
You'll demonise "gal pals" and gay men for their sexual
    "transgressions".
You will reinforce patriarchal norms and fawn over masculine
    aggression.
You will accept it that Brexit means Brexit.
Lay to bed those perplexing, progressive ethics.
You will believe the rhetoric that my paper spews and spiels is
    logical and real.'
He leaves me speechless in his ceaseless breachless beliefs.
The gulf between the ideologies of him and me
the size of a battlebus promising us £350 million for the NHS wide
    and an ocean drowning innocent immigrants deep.
A bigotry that beggars belief and demands disdain.
I simply say, 'When bigotry thrives, humanity fails.
No!
I will never believe or read the *Daily Mail*.'

BROADER BROADCASTING CORPORATION

Some days I wake up tired, uninspired and frightened
by the state of the world for young girls today.
I wake up afraid of the staggering sexism statistics
about pay gaps and age rows and lack of women in big business,
the role of the media and the portrayal of women within it.
But somebody has to fix it, to make other people listen, and that's
    the reason
I am driven to not give in to that overwhelming dread.
Instead I leave the house, get out of bed.
Because some things need to be said and somebody has to be
    the one to say them.
So today I am honestly, sonorously proclaiming this statement:
WE NEED A BROADER BROADCASTING CORPORATION.
Because it's frustrating to live in a world where we are told that
girls beneath glass ceilings should never throw stones.
Because there are not enough older women in radio and television
    in positions of power.
And if I could have it my way, every hour would be *Woman's Hour*.
Because our lives and our fights and our rights are still ignored.
Women and girls need to be brought to the fore so the force of our
    thoughts is heard MORE.
Because our cause is too important to not stick up for.
And of course,
some things are getting better.
And I know that some will dismiss this as promoting a fictitious and
    vicious agenda of gender.
But the fact is we have to endeavour to do better,
when only five percent of broadcasters' presenters are women
    over fifty,
when women of colour are a marginalised minority,
or when I speak to young girls in schools who tell me they cannot
    think of a
SINGLE. INSPIRING. FEMALE.
And the moment that we allow that is the moment that we fail.
When we let the world prevail in perpetuating a patriarchy that is
    largely
PALE
STALE
AND MALE.

So give me fewer men in suits and more Mel and Sue.
More pastry, less patriarchy.
Because it really takes the biscuit to continue to insist on forced
    gender roles for women.
Our ambitions need to take off, become greater than the
    British Bake Off.
For the sake of all of our futures:
I want to see more female writers, directors, and producers.
I want every young girl to feel that she is useful, not useless.
That she can choose what she does in the world.
That she can let her potential unfurl without fear of abuse being
    hurled at her
when she gets to the top.
But we will never get to the top unless we stop public women being
BLOCKED
AND MOCKED
AND KNOCKED DOWN THE LADDER.
We need to stop the laddish, loutish laughter at women showing
    their intelligence,
their eloquence and excellence.
We need more Kirsty Warks and more Kirsty Youngs, more role
    models for the young
showing the lives they can live and the things they can aspire to
    become.
Because our time it has come to be witty and wise and wild and
    outspoken,
to be the ones hosting flagship TV programmes.
Because putting a token woman on a panel show doesn't actually
    mean that we're in on the joke.
Our culture is still broken, still clinging insistently to ridiculous false
    notions
that women are not funny enough to be on TV,
that women do not deserve to be treated or paid equally,
that women are incapable of ever achieving equality.
And the problem isn't just on our screens, it's behind the scenes.
It's thirty-one out of thirty-eight BBC meeting rooms named after men.
It's when Google searches reduce female newsreaders to body parts
as part of the parcel of being a presenter,

whilst their male counterparts depart without their legs or the way
that they are dressed even being mentioned.
I'm tired of society so slow to learn its lesson.
And I think that it is time that we questioned
the online restless, reckless rhetoric directed at women appearing on
Question Time
or *Newsnight* or any other primetime TV show.
Because we deserve to be shown inspiring pioneers.
We deserve to learn to love the ancient world with Mary Beard.
Be schooled in the strength of women's voices by the likes of
Bonnie Greer.
We need to hear Gemma Cairney, so carefree, fresh and fierce and
feminist and fun
on Radio 1.
For we've only just begun to make women's voices more audible,
to learn from the likes of the laudable Lauren Laverne on 6 Music.
We need to celebrate our shrewdness, our fruitful irrefutable
beautifulness.
We have to stay tough.
We cannot give up until there is true diversity,
until every single girl can turn on a TV and see someone like her
who allows us all to believe, encourages the power of dreams,
enables us all to be successful and to achieve.
Because the day we will be one step closer to free is when all of us
can see
what we might want to be broadcast loudly and proudly on the BBC.

THE WORKSHOP

'We ask ourselves, "Who am I to be brilliant, gorgeous, talented, fabulous?" Actually, who are you not to be? [...] Your playing small does not serve the world.'

Marianne Williamson

She asks me, 'When will I be better?
When will I not want to write *that* letter?'
When will the sky feel wider, heart be emboldened and brighter?
When will the world begin to excite her, provide her with a life she
    can treasure?
When will the pain turn to pleasure, end the relentlessness of
    these distended despairing sentences, when will darkness desist?
'When will I be fiery, strong, and feminist like you, Miss?'
But from the midst of my own black hole,
I don't know how to heal her to whole,
make light and life shine from her shivering sunless soul.
Let hope become burrowed in her bones, make her want to exist.
From the depths of my failing ailing aching abyss,
I don't know what the answer is.
How to help her.
How to tell her about where the light lives.
I say to her, this:
Young friend, you, like I, were born to mend.
Pen it in a paragraph,
know that joy is often paved with a path built from the pain of the
    past,
this too shall pass.
This greyness, this staleness will not last.
You do not have to suffer.
Like Dorothy in Oz, your life that was can wash from greyscale to
    technicolour.
From this, your spirits can lift and your body can recover.
There is another road, a life of yellow brick gold in which you can find
health and heart and home.
Repeat after me: there's no place like hope.
There's no place like hope.
Honestly.
There's no place like hope.

'My wish for you is that you continue. Continue to be who and how you are, to astonish a mean world with your acts of kindness.'

Maya Angelou

Lightning Source UK Ltd.
Milton Keynes UK
UKOW01f0245260118
316864UK00006B/454/P